AF328376

# How to Get an Unfair Advantage

by Ethan McClean

OLD STREET PUBLISHING

First published in 2007 by Old Street Publishing Ltd,
28-32 Bowling Green Lane, London EC1R 0BJ, UK
www.oldstreetpublishing.co.uk

ISBN13: 978-1-905847-19-8

10 9 8 7 6 5 4 3 2 1



A CIP catalogue record for this book is available from the British Library.

Huge thanks to

Roy & Pauline McClean

Betley Whitehorne - especially Piet

www.getunfair.com

FIRSTLY, PUT ANY HONESTY, CONSCIENCE, VIRTUE OR INTEGRITY ASIDE IN A VERY SAFE PLACE

THEN...

HEDGE YOUR BETS

BRIBE THE GROUNDSMAN

TURN ON THE CHARM

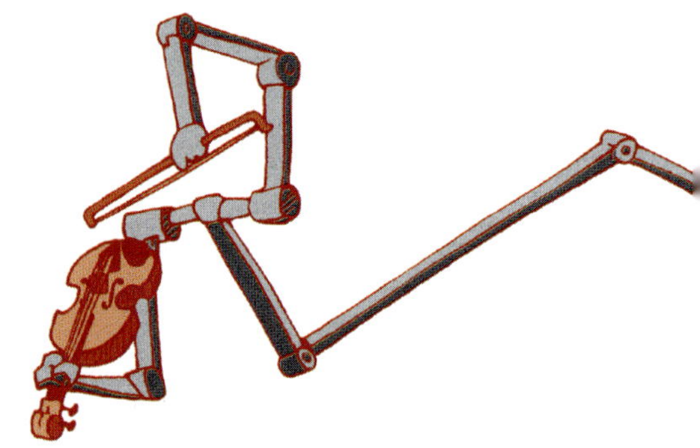

# FLYPAPER

UNLEASH THE SHIP'S TERMITE

AUDITION VISHNU

UTILISE

# YOUR NATURAL ASSETS

...OR SOMEONE ELSE'S

FOR STAN THE BELL TOLLS
STANLEYPEDIA
D-K
WAR & PEACE & STAN
STANLEY & THE CHOCOLATE FACTORY
STAN EYRE
THE DA STANLEY CODE
101 WAYS TO COOK STAN

BREAK INTO THE PRINTERS

FIND A CORPORATE SPONSOR
FOR YOUR FACELIFT

KEEP ABREAST OF THE
LATEST FASHIONS

# TRAIN

76

DILIGENTLY WORK
YOUR WAY UP THE
LADDER FROM THE
LOWLIEST RUNG

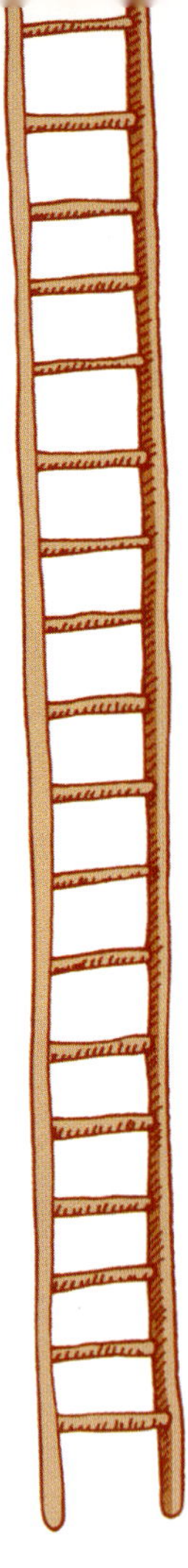

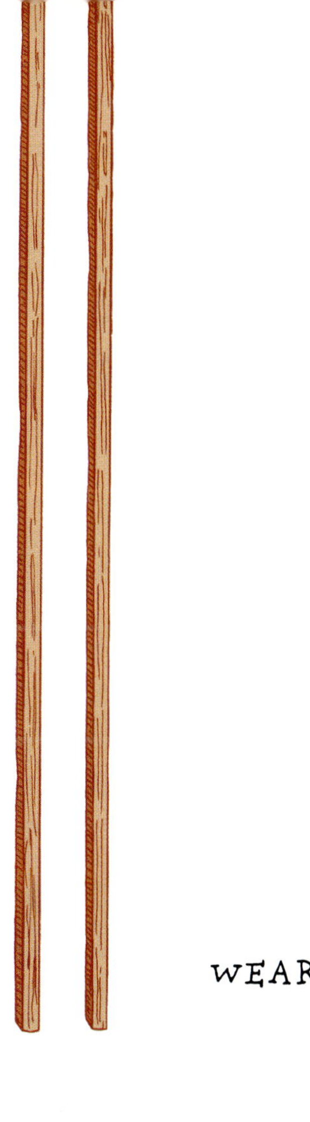

WEAR STILTS

PICK JIM...

...AND PUT HIM IN GOAL

COPYRIGHT SOMETHING
REALLY USEFUL

FOUND F.U.R.S.

(THE FELINE UPTREE RESCUE SERVICE)

ROLL UP A SOCK

CONCEIVE A CHILD PRODIGY

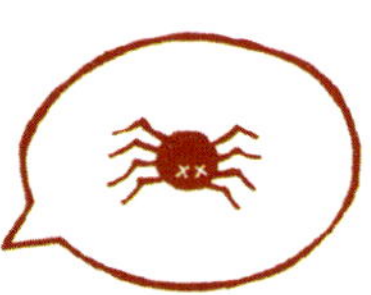

THE GNATTER

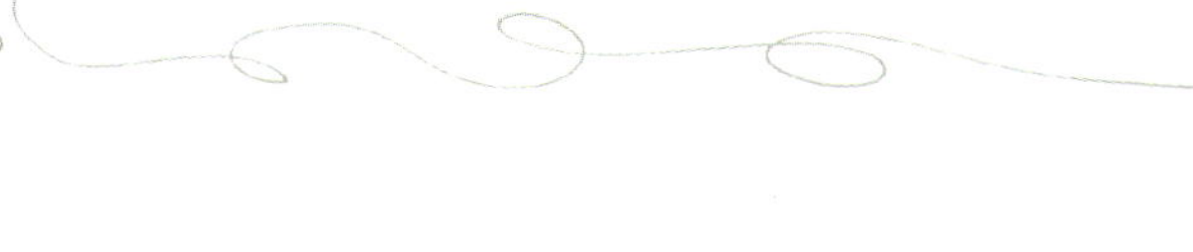

# LEARN INSECT

STRAP TWO FISH TO YOUR FEET

FLAUNT YOUR DECADENT AND OSTENTATIOUS SIDE...

...WHILE KEEPING YOUR MEAN
AND MISERLY SIDE TO YOURSELF

ALWAYS TAKE THE PISTOL

STEAL THE MOST TALENTED OF
RICHARD CLAYDERMAN'S FINGERS

MAKE A PRE-EMPTIVE STRIKE

# BEFRIEND A LUMBERJACK

OR A ROCKET SCIENTIST

MARRY SOMEONE IMPORTANT

# DETONATE THE QUEUE

WRITE THE DIRECTIONS UNDER

YOUR EYELIDS

DISCOVER A
NEW CONTINENT

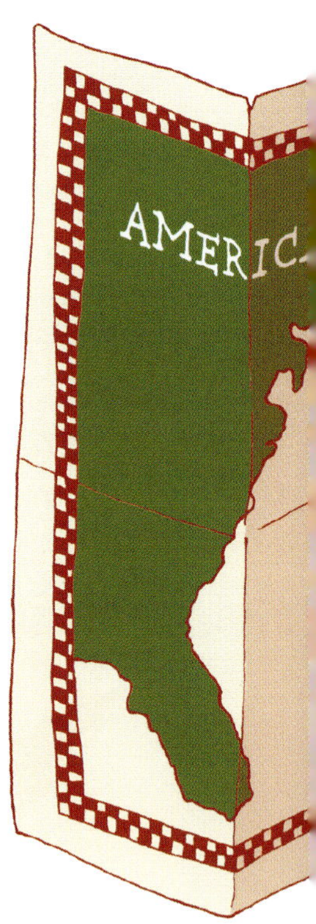

ALAN
EUROPE
N
THE MAP

COINCIDE YOUR CEILING CLEANING WITH NEXT DOOR'S SÉANCE NIGHT

SYNCHRONISE SÉANCE NIGHT
WITH NEXT DOOR'S MAGNET CLUB

START A FAMILY BUSINESS

TAPE TARANTULAS
TO YOUR TOES

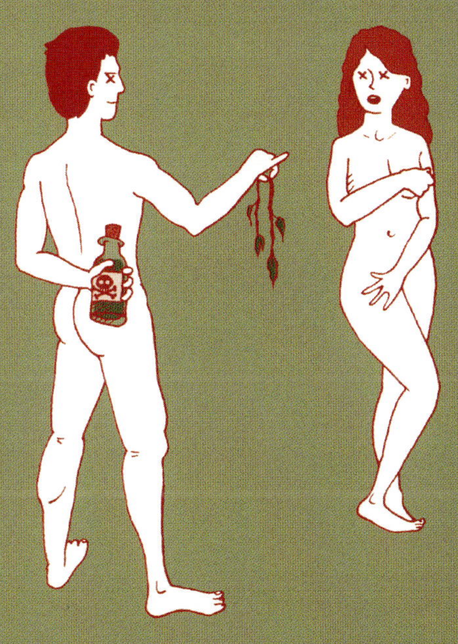

INFORM EVE OF THE
FIG TREE'S DEMISE

WANTED
BLACK BOOT
BILLY
$10,000

# SUPERGLUE

STEAL A GREAT IDEA

DRAW ATTENTION TO
YOUR EROGENOUS ZONES
WITH LUMINOUS PAINT

PICK ON SOMETHING
SMALLER THAN YOU

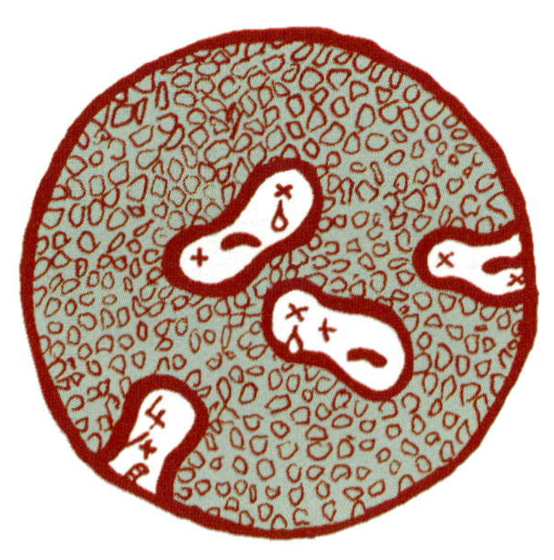

SELL YOUR GRANNY

TURN YOUR
TROUSER-PRESS
UP TO MAX

DEPLOY THE TEE-MAESTRO-3000

# TRAIN A LION

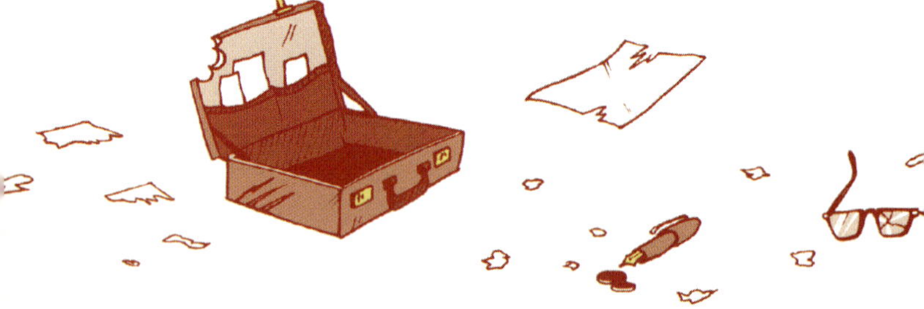

TO LIAISE WITH THE TAX MAN

DONORS
ONLY

POPULATE THE PLANET
WITH YOUR DNA

GROW YOUR BRAIN TO
ENORMOUS PROPORTION

UNIONISE

LEARN TO SURVIVE IN THE WILD

NAME
*********
PWD
*****

# PASSWORD PROTECT YOUR HANDBAG

SNEAK A STATUE
OF YOURSELF INTO
THE MUSEUM

GO FOR LUCKY SEVEN DURING AN INSECT INFESTATION

DUPLICATE YOURSELF WITH CARDBOARD AND NEVER ATTEND ANOTHER MEETING

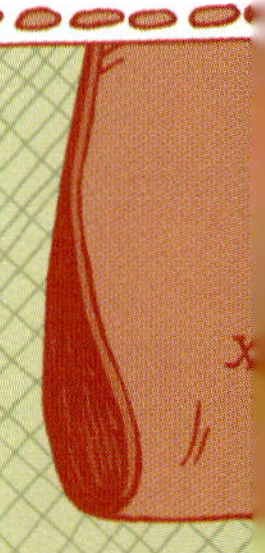

SEW TWO NAME TAGS INTO YOUR PANTS

RGE

...IN CASE YOU LOSE THEM TWICE

FINALLY REVEAL YOUR SUPERPOWER

FIGHT DIRTY WHEN
YOU WRESTLE WITH
YOUR CONSCIENCE

BUY IN BULK

**bělch,** *v.i.* & *t.* emit wind noisily from stomach through mouth; (of volcano, gun, &c.) emit fire, smoke, &c. *n.* belching; eructation.

EAT A DICTIONARY

TURN THE TABLES

ATTAIN A BLACKBELT

KING-FU
DAILY

PAINT YOUR GIRAFFE BROWN

PRETEND TO BE MORE DISADVANTAGED THAN YOU ACTUALLY ARE

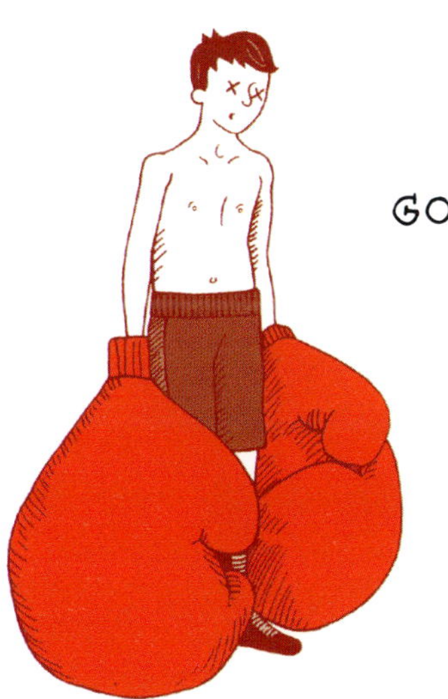

GO LARGE

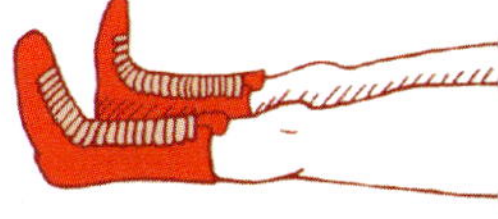

FILL YOUR RUCKSACK WITH HELIUM

EDUCATE YOURSELF
IN TRAJECTORY

COME
ARMAGEDDON,
BE AWAY
ON BUSINESS

INVEST IN A LUCK HARNESS

CUSTOMER
SERVICES
WHEN YOU MEET YOUR MAKER,
DEMAND A REFUND